THE
Crayola
COMPARING SIZES
BOOK

JODIE SHEPHERD

LERNER PUBLICATIONS ◆ MINNEAPOLIS

TO MY FAMILY: THOUGH YOU ARE ALL TALLER THAN ME—I AM THE SHORTEST—I LOVE YOU.

Official Licensed Product
Lerner Publications Company
A division of Lerner Publishing Group, Inc.
241 First Avenue North
Minneapolis, MN 55401 USA

For reading levels and more information, look up this title at www.lernerbooks.com.

Main body text set in Billy Infant Regular 24/30.
Typeface provided by SparkyType.

Library of Congress Cataloging-in-Publication Data

Names: Shepherd, Jodie, author.
Title: The Crayola comparing sizes book / by Jodie Shepherd.
Description: Minneapolis : Lerner Publications, [2018] | Series: Crayola concepts | Audience: Age 4-9. | Audience: K to grade 3. | Includes bibliographical references and index.
Identifiers: LCCN 2016049257 (print) | LCCN 2016050359 (ebook) | ISBN 9781512432893 (lb : alk. paper) | ISBN 9781512455670 (pb : alk. paper) | ISBN 9781512449235 (eb pdf)
Subjects: LCSH: Size perception—Juvenile literature. | Crayons—Juvenile literature.
Classification: LCC BF299.S5 S53424 2018 (print) | LCC BF299.S5 (ebook) | DDC 153.7/52—dc23

LC record available at https://lccn.loc.gov/2016049257

Manufactured in the United States of America
1-41820-23780-3/7/2017

Table of Contents

DIFFERENT SIZES ALL AROUND

Everything has a size. Size is how large or small something is. Buttons come in many sizes. So do toys and shapes and even people.

COMPARING

When we compare, we find what's alike and different. Tomatoes can be different sizes.

One tomato is big. The other is small.

You can draw the same shape in different sizes. Try it!

Some animals are tall. Others are short.

With its long neck, the giraffe eats leaves from tall trees.

The short zebra feeds on grass.

MANY SIZES

Thin brushes create thin lines. Wide brushes create wider lines.

Thin lines are smaller. Wide lines are bigger. Use different brushes to make thin and wide lines.

Which of these colored pencils are long?
Which are short?

The more you draw with your pencils and crayons, the shorter they become.

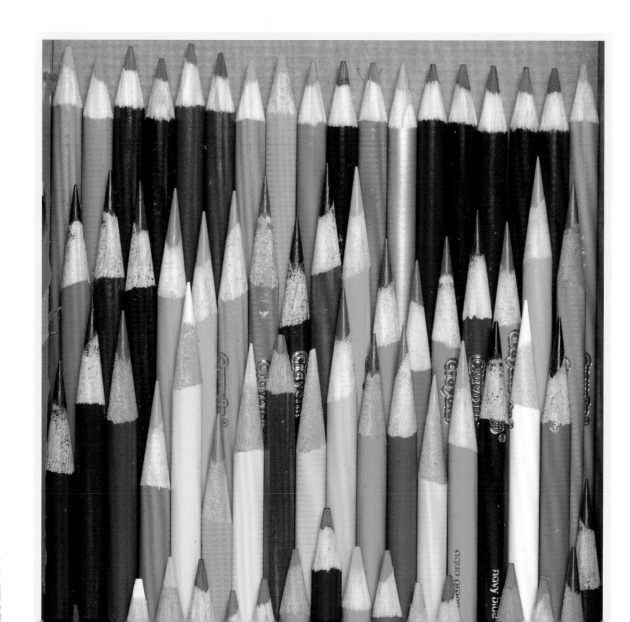

Little nesting dolls fit into bigger . . . and bigger . . . and bigger nesting dolls.

Make a picture by drawing small shapes inside bigger shapes.

Arranging boots from tallest to shortest makes it easy to see how their sizes are different.

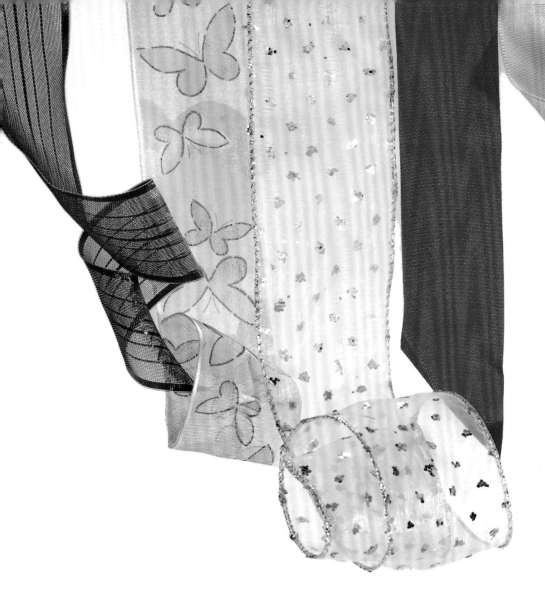

Ribbons come in many lengths. They can be long, short, or anywhere in between!

Try drawing curly lines. What is the longest curly line you can make?

Look around you. How many different sizes can you find?

WORLD OF COLORS

Here are some of the Crayola® crayon colors used in this book. Can you find them in the photos? You can draw pictures in all kinds of sizes and colors!

SPRING GREEN

WILD STRAWBERRY

RADICAL RED

NEON CARROT

MAGENTA

CARIBBEAN GREEN

GREEN YELLOW

TIMBERWOLF

GLOSSARY

arranging: putting in a certain order

compare: to look at two or more things closely to see what is alike or what is different about them

length: how long something is

nesting doll: a wooden doll in a set of dolls that get smaller in size and fit one inside another

thin: short from side to side

wide: long from side to side

TO LEARN MORE

BOOKS

Barner, Bob. *Ants Rule: The Long and Short of It*. New York: Holiday House, 2017. Read this fun story about how a group of ants planning for a bug carnival learn about size and measurement.

May, Eleanor. *Albert's Bigger Than Big Idea*. New York: Kane, 2013. Learn more about comparing big and small in this book!

Shepherd, Jodie. *The Crayola Sorting Book*. Minneapolis: Lerner Publications, 2017. After comparing sizes, read about how you might sort objects by size and more!

WEBSITES

Building Boxes
http://www.crayola.com/crafts/building-boxes-craft/
Create boxes to store your things in or use them to wrap gifts. You can make them in many sizes—and even stack them inside one another!

Time to Compare
https://www.turtlediary.com/game/comparing-objects.html
Play this game to practice comparing sizes.

PHOTO ACKNOWLEDGMENTS

The images in this book are used with the permission of: © iStockphoto.com/Victorburnside, p. 5 (top left); © Dmussman/Shutterstock.com, p. 5 (top right); © Choneschones/Dreamstime.com, p. 5 (bottom left); © iStockphoto.com/wanderluster, p. 5 (bottom right); © Cre8tive Images/Shutterstock.com, p. 5 (center); © iStockphoto.com/Upyanose, p. 6; © Yoko Design/Shutterstock.com, p. 7 (background border); © Africa Studio/Shutterstock.com, p. 8; © iStockphoto.com/anankkml, p. 9; © Alexandru Nika/Shutterstock.com, p. 10; © Ilya Martynov/Shutterstock.com, p. 11 (background border); © Todd Strand/Independent Picture Service, pp. 12, 13; © iStockphoto.com/ibreakstock, p. 14; © bosotochka/Shutterstock.com, p. 15 (background border); © iStockphoto.com/petrenkod, p. 17; © Westend61/SuperStock, p. 18; © Paket/Shutterstock.com, p. 19 (background border); © iStockphoto.com/leonori, p. 20; © iStockphoto.com/shoo_arts, p. 21 (top left); © iStockphoto.com/brozova, p. 21 (top right); © iStockphoto.com/paulprescott72, p. 21 (bottom left); © Ron Chapple/Dreamstime.com, p. 21 (bottom right); © iStockphoto.com/Tuned_In, p. 21 (center).

Cover: © iStockphoto.com/gpointstudio (girls); © Ocusfocus/Dreamstime.com (shoes); © Todd Strand/Independent Picture Service (pencils); © Vadim Usov/Dreamstime.com (candy).